Journey in the Mind's Eye of a Poet: A Search for Faith

Book Six (2011 to 2012)

Another Day

Tony Prewit

Journey in the Mind's Eye of a Poet: A Search for Faith
Book Six (2011 to 2012): Another Day
copyright Tony Prewit, 2012

Published by Ridgeline Press
Silver City, New Mexico, U.S.A.
ISBN 978-0-9854487-5-2

Editing, book design, cover design, and production services by
Heidi Connolly, Harvard Girl Word Services
Cover artwork by Tony Prewit

Acknowledgments

I would like to thank my wife, Patricia Prewit, for the years of assistance in sorting, editing, and proofreading all my work. I thank her most of all for her being her and allowing me to continue to be the person she married. I would also like to thank Sarah Johnson, a professional proofreader, who offered intelligent suggestions in shaping these books and gave me a valuable critique of its quality and content. Finally, I would like to thank the friends who read the complete series, contributed valuable suggestions, and urged me to arrange it into the form it has become: Gretchen Van Auken, Charlie Mckee, and Gail Rein. I thank Raymond Hornbaker for the years of commitment to our late-night discussions. I would also like to mention the editor who helped with the final sculpture of these books, Heidi Connolly, whose vision, talent, and professional guidance have been invaluable.

Table of Contents

Prologue

These six books are written in a poetry/prose form, a process that spans thirty-five years and encompasses the gradual evolution into my inner search for a personal faith and belief in God. It is a poet's journal and also like a novel in poetry form, one in which I am the narrator as well as a main character. The poems document my gradual disengagement with traditional, conservative, evangelical Christianity as I built a belief and faith of my own. Although I certainly did not have this defined purpose when I started this journal, it matured this way over time to become collection of six books that record a journey in search of a faith I could call my own.

As I walk away from the Christianity in which I once believed without doubting the existence of a God, I continue to discover a place within where I am learning how to build my own faith. This writing is for those who are at a dead end or a crossroad in their belief, or in a dysfunctional relationship (so to speak) with their spiritual beliefs. One of my messages, therefore, is that our spiritual beliefs do not have to be unchangeable.

Consequently, these poems are not so much a criticism of Christianity as they are a process of learning to ask the right questions. Over time I have learned to be wary of those who do not want to hear my questions and who are defensive toward honest doubt and inquiry. Because I was trapped in a doctrine that did not allow me to express my belief in my own way, and because I wanted to keep my Christian friends, I kept silent for many years.

The poems in this work capture my observations and reflections about how I see life through the veil of my own struggle, and will hopefully allow others to consider the shortcomings of their own beliefs, or of any belief that does not allow for true dialog. Because none of us really knows the truth for sure when it comes to belief, it would appear that there are shortcomings in all spiritual belief systems, regardless of form. For that reason, we are left to ourselves to construct a satisfactory — and satisfying — faith.

The stunning effect of this pursuit is my finding that God gets larger from the inside out. This is where my journey has found its pleasure and its peace, even while admitting the sorrow and fear of the search.

I have wrestled with my soul along this path and it wrestled back, for what I was struggling with was my spiritual identity. In wrestling, I learned the value of putting forth the right questions rather than assuming I had the right answers.

In fact, questions have become answers in their own right for me, for a light turned on in the asking that helped illuminate my way. I further learned that without questions we have no way to really appreciate where we are going and why. As such, I am thankful that I realized the importance of questions within the arena of spiritual beliefs.

The six books in this series are (in order): *Journal of Time, Portals and Passages, The Book of the Lost and Found* or *Chasing Rainbows, Moods of War, The Source,* and *Another Day.*

Book One is the beginning of my realizations and observations of life, which I describe as "me looking inside me from the perspective of the outside me," and then, "me looking outside me from the perspective of the inside me." It is the discovery of my need for a faith in God of my own. Book Two is a confession of my dreams and the effect dreams can have upon one's life. Book Two also reveals my earliest thoughts concerning my spiritual beliefs, kept very secret until then, and how these secrets became a burden to my search for faith. In Books Three and Four I begin to focus my writing toward a more intense spiritual inquiry based on my discontentment with religious answers. These two works became like a great mountain I needed to climb, blocking the path of what I considered my "true" journey. One might also describe them as an inner wrestling match where the rule was to fight to the finish. In total these books are the recording of how I lost my past faith and discovered what I call "conflicts of faith." Hence, Book Five is the result of feeling as if I had reached the top of the mountain, had a good view of a long way down the road, and could tell that although the journey was long from over, I was sensing a peace that came from finding my own faith. Book Six is about learning to live with the faith I had created.

Phrases and Words

The phrase "Treat others as we want them to treat us" is the most frequently used phrase in these books, and it has become more important to me as the years have passed. It has become a part of the foundation of my own faith because no matter how I might try, it stuck with me, withstanding all inquiry, doubt, and question.

To treat others as we want them to treat us simply means to me that we value others as equal to ourselves and value their needs as important as our own. And that if we do not wish to be cheated, lied to, deceived, oppressed, or manipulated, then we should be willing not to cheat, lie, deceive, oppress, or manipulate others.

I use other Judeo-Christian terms such as "heaven" and "hell" and the duality of "good" and "evil." These terms and their meanings come from my own culture and western traditional Christian teaching. I do not necessarily consider these terms to be universally accepted as truth; they serve only as my own points of reference into my inner spiritual search.

My use of the word "God" in the masculine form is habit and based somewhat on the limitations of the English language. In my mind, God is of no gender, no religion, no race, no culture.

In some parts you may find the writing in these books somewhat redundant. The repetitiveness serves as an accurate picture of my perspective, however, for I believe we are all in the process of being formed and we repeat our thoughts and feelings until they either become a part of us or fade.

My style of writing is varied. It weaves poetry, commentary, and prose. I do not attempt to stay inside the lines of strict grammatical compliance. I give myself poetic license. I am much more concerned with content and the work's original form than with adherence to rules. You'll see I have also invented a few words along the way.

Initially, my poetry/journal was not produced as a neat stack of notebooks; instead, scattered notebooks, legal pads, single sheets, and scratch paper filled with writings piled up until the notebooks piled up on top of each other. They were in no real order. No, I did not have a neat stack at all. In fact, after thirty-five years' worth of notebooks had turned into a kind of organizational nightmare, I felt it was almost futile to even attempt to sort through it all. Common sense prevailed, however, and this six-book format is the result of sorting and compiling a presentable record of my writings.

Part One:
Another Day

The Need for Connection

as i see it
most people have a need to connect to a God
without having to be told
— as if the need is innate

> *but if this is so*
> *then why is God so elusive on the issue?*

Where Is This God

1.

the early morning is cool
but not cold
with a slight breeze
and quiet

mornings like this
are the first signs of spring

> *my thoughts are on myself*
> *as i imagine i am reaching out*
> *to the Power that made us*

> *i want to be heard*
> *and i want the Power to move on my behalf*
> *and i want answers*

the time before the sun peeks over the horizon
is the time i believe the Power is listening
and is willing to prove its existence

the loneliest time is when i have needs so justified
but receive no answers

so i am up at dawn searching for this Power
that does not answer

> *and with every sunrise*
> *comes another day*
> *like the one before.*

2.

i wrestle with a resentment that is barely recognizable
and my anger is fed by a helplessness in me
that continues to reach for the Power

my loneliness rises up in me with each sunrise
and i wear a mask of joy to hide my feelings

my real face is of despair with every first light
for only then am i willing to believe
the Power will bring the miracle i need

> *but with every sunrise*
> *comes another day*
> *like the one before.*

3.

the paradox of this failed expectation
is the solace i find every morning in the sunrise

though the Power fails to answer my need
the sunrise does minister to my emptiness
but not for long

though i truly enjoy nature in the mornings
i am not satisfied
though nature ministers to my inner self
it does not heal my broken body

i believe the Power can heal
but that it does not
so who do i blame
— me or the Power?

so with every sunrise
comes another day
like the one before . . .

how long am i expected to believe in the Power like
this?
is God's sunrise better for me than my need of
healing?

Another Day

1.

the number of the most deserving people
who have the most undeserved tragedies in their lives
is a high enough number to cause me to wonder
about the real involvement of God
based on whether the merit of our lives
deserves God's protection.

2.

it is another day and i am dealing with it
on the terms of how life is dealt
seemingly without the regard
of a God who is there
for those who are deserving and in need.

3.

the chores keep piling up
another day keeps coming
and we are left with no real answers
yet we are still willing to believe in a God
who loves us and cares for us
and will protect us from harm.

As I Remember It (49 years later)

pecos texas
september 1960
at the house of one of my parents' friends
i am outside playing alone while my parents are visiting

i do not know where my brother is or the two sons of my
parents' friends
i am in the backyard where the grass is high and a porch
light shines

the mosquitoes are out and the air is wet
in the grass lie the "stilts" that my brother and the other
boys have made

the small ones i had mastered quickly
but lying in the grass now i see the taller stilts and am
drawn to them immediately

i pick them up clumsily and balance myself on the steps of
the back porch
i place my feet into the straps and after a few short
awkward steps i go lunging to the ground

my knee — i forget which one — hits a sharp rock and i
stand up quickly in case anyone has seen
i will blame my fall on the mosquitoes swarming
around me as i made my attempt

but there is something more pressing to attend —
my knee is throbbing and some skin is missing
the tissue under the skin is red and blood and other liquids
are seeping out

i run up the back steps and into the kitchen interrupting
the chatter of the grown-ups
my mom and dad look at the wound quickly and ask
what happened

i do not tell them exactly leaving out the part of my
aborted journey on the tall stilts
my mom hands me a wet towel and says *be more careful*

i go back outside
i hear the grownups laughing
i am not sure if they are laughing at me or
at one of their stories

back outside with a throbbing knee i swat at the
mosquitoes and wait
it seems an eternity before my parents are ready to leave

then my brother and the other boys show up unconcerned
about my wound and me.

> *the lesson?*
> *when one wants to grow up too quickly*
> *the fall can really hurt*
> *or…*
> *be content with the small stilts in life*
> *before attempting the higher ones.*

Born To

1.

are we born to reach for gods
and born not to know?

are we born to believe in gods (or not)
and born to faith without conclusions?

2.

body and mind and heart and spirit fail me not
in my walk with what is unknown
may my last breath be at peace
with all the unanswered questions.

3.

there is mystery in our future beyond this life
for the gods keep the mystery to themselves

i can only hope that if our destiny be in
the hands of the gods
that they will keep it safe.

4.

are we born to this earth not to know
and born to strive?

is justice ours to mete out as we see it?
if we err how is the error fixed?

5.

i look as far down the road of life as i can
if as i go i bump into one of the gods
it is up to me to remember not to rely on them for much.

Long Enough

How can we learn to enjoy preparing ourselves for tomorrow knowing there is always work yet to be done?

The temptation to choose ease and reject work can destroy us.

Like pedaling uphill, if we stay with it we will make it to the top, but if we stop the hill does not come to us.

Perhaps knowing the next hill will be easier because we made it up the first hill helps us in our daily tasks.

Therefore, if life is seen as a series of hills we must pedal, and if we can find some meaning and joy in making it up each hill, then perhaps our effort could produce a some meaning and joy in our life — if we stay with it long enough.

An 82-year-old Woman Named Lou

She played the violin and traveled the world. At our first meeting she shared that she was in awe of the world and the universe and everything around her more than she had ever been before.

She said that real knowledge admits what it does not know and that she recognizes the real seekers because they can admit what they do not know.

After this greeting she quietly picked up her violin and began to softly bring forth some of the most beautiful melodies I had ever heard.

Though she could have studied with the masters and the greats she preferred to spend her time gardening and playing with her grandchildren.

There was a sparkle in her eyes.

How it got there and how long it had been there I do not know but I do know it was there.

she had the face of wisdom and the eyes of a child
my wife and i loved her immediately.

Grass in the Wind

a soft breeze
sweeps across
the tops of the
grass

you and i
are there
lying on the
greenery

the current
plays amidst
our embrace

> *grass in the wind*
> *bring your passion*
> *we are ready*
> *and willing*
> *to begin*

sunsets
and clouds
color the
sky

the sky
the canvas
the clouds
the brushes

sunsets
the colors of light
painted on
the horizon

you and i
lying under
the painted
sky

sunset and clouds
bring your desire
we are ready
and willing
to begin.

I Am More Alone

i am more alone in a city full of people
than in a stretch of desert
with hardly a living thing in the vicinity. . . .

why is that?

I Gave My Time

i gave my time and energy today
to someone who needed it

    i sense my spirit is pleased

my life is defined by my knowing how to help others
and knowing the peace it gives

    i sense my spirit is pleased

when i wake in the mornings i feel my spirit is a cover for
me
and if i die tomorrow or live many years i know without a
doubt

    my spirit is pleased.

A Man's Face

1.

i looked away
for only a moment
it seems
  and you were gone

you said it was
years coming
and you said
  it was too late

you said i had changed
and you said
  you had changed

i can hardly believe
i had this talk with you
in the
  front doorway

you closed the
door on me
the door to the house
we had built.

2.

love cannot stay the same
like a seed it requires of us the desire
to care for it
—and then it has a chance to bloom

if my love could bloom again till death do us part
— then we could part with the knowledge
and privilege of knowing we succeeded
at love again.

3.

i cannot call my love back
even with this new found wisdom

i must walk this new place in life
and hope i have time to find love again.

I See

i see no hell in the heavens
i see no God who needs to punish

i see a God who watches over us and lets us rule the earth
with little intervention

i see a God who has placed a part of Himself in us
and that we are to seek God there

i see a God who can be found in each of us where
we learn what God does and does not do in our lives

i see a God who neither rewards nor punishes
but allows us to reward and punish ourselves

> *if we cannot find a better way to peace*
> *then reward and punishment are compromises*
> *to the way of peace*

i see a God who allows us to be burdened with the evil of
our own making
which is hell enough for us

> *could it be that we are here to look after ourselves*
> *and that we are accountable to ourselves while on the earth*
> *and that when we die God will look after us?*

> *could it be that it is not God but we who hate and punish*
> *and that God takes us on to the next journey*
> *where hell is not an option?*

as i contemplate these questions i do not really see
that much will ever change
for there are many who cling to the idea
that God must punish and reward
to the idea that we know all there is to know
and who do not see the paradox
in the fact that their neighbors feel the same way
— that they themselves are the ones who know
and that we are the ones who need to change

hence i see a God who allows us to war
and destroy ourselves
over such an absurd and unnecessary belief in His name

> *so all the days become just another day for heaven and earth*
> *as we wallow in the insistence that there is a heaven and a*
> *hell waiting for us after our life here on earth is done . . .*

> *and we fight over who has the rights to decide which*
> *belief is right.*

Jesus Theology

1.

i lay my Christian hat down
and i pick up another one
that fits me better

God allows me to come to Him
as i am and i am not
turned away

perhaps we all go to "heaven"
and God guides us by
our spirits

No *one* belief owns
the truth about God.

2.

Jesus was only one of the ones who shared the message
"treat others how you want them to treat you"

> *. . . do not cheat, lie, or oppress others*
> *see their life as equal to your own*
> *be willing to show compassion toward*
> *those in need.*

3.

the jesus theology is not owned by him
it was not first conceived by him
he is one of many

and the message is for anyone
who comprehends its value.

Coming to Terms with Three Thoughts

1.
hear me out God —
i am not content
with the failure
of the promises
of the jesus
theology

hear me out God —
You have not
told us
why we have failed
to find You
nor where to
look for
You

hear me out God —
in Your silence
we come
to find You
and we leave
empty
but
we imagine
we have
found
You

hear me out God —
i have surmised by
Your silence that
You are not a

disapproving
God

but rather that Your
silence
is approval
and you condemn
us not

therefore
if we reach for You
and imagine that You
need a savior
for us

Your silence accepts
our need for a
savior
accepts the
failure of
our belief
as if it
matters
not

is Your silence
a clue to Your decision
about what happens
to us after we die?

does Your silence say
the decision has
already been
made?

hear me out God —
is it in Your silence
You expect us to be at peace
with these issues?
is it up to us to look
and know what
needs to be done
in order for us
to coexist?

hear me out God —
i believe You are impartial
and that every life receives
from You equally
in regard to
the spirit

is the good news that we need not
be concerned with life after death
but rather life as it now?

    2.
hear me out God —
because i
have believed
in the unseen God
and the unheard God
i am now a person of faith
and i am righteous in Your sight

as to how i come to You and why
and what i believe our relationship is
it all seems important
only because i am the one doing the asking

does my belief in You make me a better human being
by forming in me the understanding
that i should value all of Your created humans
as equal to myself?

do i care about others as i do about myself?

do You make Yourself known
by the questions we ask?

3.
hear me out God –
is our closeness to You
seen in our understanding
of the value of every human being
and living thing on the earth?

are there many paths
to this one truth
and can we find this truth
on many paths?

I Silently Weep

i silently weep till i am drained
then i wait till i am filled again
i silently weep again
till i am drained again
and i repeat this
again and
again

the audacity of humans is unfathomable
carrying their belief like swords
believing all who are different
to be enemies of God
and truth

i silently weep for the tragedy that is in the lives
that miss the real beauty of God
in a place where no one
is turned
away.

Just Another Day for the Raven

the raven in flight
is a familiar sight
in southwest new mexico

i have watched many a raven
scout the skies for its prey
as its silhouette floats in harmony against
a distant horizon

i make no analogies here for it is just another day
in southwest new mexico
where nature still plays a part

i would miss the ravens if they were gone
but being they are not
it is just another day for the ravens.

Southwest New Mexico Contemplation

i am on top of a barren hill
i am looking out onto a vast prairie
no one is around
i can see for miles and miles

it is here in a place like this where one can take a chance
to explore the depths within

but beware for the aloneness of these deserts can convince
one of almost anything

many religions have been conceived in places like this

truth and lies
show no favorites.

Much of the Southwest (June 2009)

At first look, much of the landscape of southwestern New Mexico is barren, but if one takes time to observe more closely, the land comes alive.

The subtle colors of grass and scrub and wildflower and cactus and rock and earth paints the land against a pale blue sky and wispy clouds. The quietude is interrupted only by wind gusts and locusts.

Take a walk and scour the earth for the movement of the animals. See how the land is a highway of insects and lizards and rabbits and birds, and know that perhaps a snake or a coyote will appear.

Feel the silence and vastness that reaches into the soul and wonder at the mystery of creation. Realize the puzzle that we are and ask all the unanswered questions.

Then return to this landscape over and over to find a peace that resides within, a peace without quarrel with God or the unknown. Find the intrigue of this mystery and the quiet way that opens you for your search for God in this expanse of southwestern New Mexico.

a raven flew by
observing me for a moment
then passing over me
i was not its next meal

as if God had told the raven at birth
what is and what is not for dinner.

40-Day Fast

1.

I read in a book about the history of monasteries. There was a quote by a monk who was fasting that went something like this: "My ribs are like the rafters in the sanctuary of the church." This inspired me to do a fast.

As I fasted I wondered if I would have the same sensation as the monk. I have to admit, I do not think I experienced feeling my ribs with the same spiritual reverence he had; however, my ribs did become fascinating to me, where I spent much time rubbing my fingers across them. In fact, they became like a rosary to me instead of the rafters of the church. I suppose one has to fast and feel one's own ribs before an image arrives.

This was my experience with my ribs and fasting.

2.

As the days wore on I had less to say and more concern about how to make it through the day. I contemplated how I would be able to get up and go about my day without wasting the energy I needed.

I was learning how to be grateful for what I had.

3.

About the tenth day into the fast I began to feel as if I could go on forever . . . I noticed that during a hike in the forest the mosquitoes left me alone, where my wife was bothered all day by the bloodsuckers. I wanted to sit and meditate in the forest, but my wife wanted to keep moving.

Peace can be elusive even while we are seemingly pursuing the most spiritual of paths.

4.

By the end of the fast I had had enough of it. I discovered that I much prefer finding God through treating others the way I want to be treated than finding God through fasting.

Perhaps God does give us choices.

The "R" Factor

My friend's testimony goes something like this:

"I see myself as the example of the one who lives as Christ intended.

"I am an educated American man who has had his share of ups and downs.

"Because I pray I have learned to receive from God through prayer.

"My family is from several generations of Christians, and God has continually anointed that history through me and my family.

"My family after me will have the same blessing from God because we have been faithful for more than a hundred years."

how does R know this to be true?
he says God has shown him and that his life proves it
i do not have the heart to tell him
how insensitive he is to others and how arrogant
he does not see in himself these traits
all he sees is a magnificent man of God

still R is indeed a remarkable and honest man
someone i would trust with any possession
and his view of himself is easily forgivable
for it is his honesty that makes up for the arrogance
and it is his honesty and character i value in his friendship.

The Ass Poem

if you ass me
asses can be friends with other asses
and most likely
that is the only acceptable kind of friend
an ass can truly ever have
for if an ass accepts another ass as a friend
this has the making of a remarkable friendship.

Ass Poem Addendum

i doubt we will make it
there has been too much failure
and i have faith in my doubt

*doubt can have a meaningful understanding
when discussing asses and friendships.*

Many Paths

1.

i stumble through the thick brush and thorns
on the path i imagine i am making
for myself to heaven

the well-worn paths have never satisfied me
so i dare to venture off alone

every idea of how God is and how He relates to us
is not known for certain
yet these ideas of God have made many well-worn
paths to heaven

and many people over the ages
have traveled these paths
as if they knew for sure they were true

> *i venture to say that my own path*
> *is as good as any other*
> *and mine satisfies my soul*
> *more than any other*
> *i have tried.*

2.

my path is one of mercy
and spiritual tolerance
for us all

from where i stand
i see God as a God of mercy and tolerance
for all His creation is without need of punishment

i believe our spirits are without flaw or blemish
and it is there where we find God
and there is where
my path leads

i believe God allows us the freedom to make our own paths.

January Night 1978

i called you by name

you were the one i wanted

you called me by name

i was the one you wanted

we recognized each other
when we saw each other for the first time

and on that january night
i took your hand in mine and never let go.

Love Bumps

our daily routine
bumps us
into each other

we lean into
the *bumps*
and linger

we brush our bodies
against each other
and slowly pass

we mark our territory
and then continue
our daily routine

these *bumps*
are the love notes
we pass to each other
every day

without love *bumps*
we would miss
each
other
terribly.

Forever in High School

1.

Our way of relating to the opposite sex seems to reach maturity at about high-school age. Though we may change somewhat after high school as we mature socially, educationally, career-wise and physically, at their core our relationships don't seem to change much at all.

Though we become more aware — learn how to court and how to love and how to commit — our initial contact still reminds me of high school.

My wife and I are 55. When we first met 32 years ago we acted like high-school kids, and when our single friends today start to date it is as if they are back in high school.

Our sexual mentality appears to peak at about 18. Why is that?

2.

I suggested this to a few friends, one of whom thought the idea childish. But with all due respect, his response sounded just as it did when we were in high school.

I Watched from a Distance

1.

they turned their heads to each other
as if guided
they eyed each other up and down and through
wondering at the other

> *i have waited too long to want to start over*
> *i have waited too long not to want to jump in*

> *i fear my loneliness will cause me to jump in*
> *at almost any opportunity*

> *though my youthful love blinded me once*
> *i survived it*
> *and now this lonely love is blinding me again*
> *and i do not know if*
> *i can survive it*

then came the mutual smiles and nods of approval
he moved sideways toward her
and she leaned toward him

i could see what i thought was a verbal exchange
and a slow tear rolled down my eye

i thought *i want them to be right for each other*
as i would for myself.

2.

two hours later . . .
they are now holding hands like children before puberty
the feeling of knowing where they are in life
mutually shared not in words
but in the holding of hands

they are for each other like a light for loneliness
and who knows
maybe in time they will grow
into their second puberty and enjoy many good days

the elderly man and woman stood in the park about 15 feet apart
then turned toward each other to find love had not
left them after all.

Shelley's Funeral

Observations . . .

    1.
only twenty or so people attended

the pallbearers looked rough
from the school of hard knocks

shelley was 52 and headstrong

she overdosed on drugs just when
things were starting to look their best

shelley was also fun-loving

her laughter was contagious and
she had a smile for you always in place

yet her depression swallowed her jocularity.

    2.
as it turns out the tough-looking pallbearers
were gentle and kind and shared
how together they'd become drug-free
and how shelley had been the center of their strength

shelley's partner shared how he and shelley
opened their home to many
in a voice with a kindness to it and drew you in

he wept for the love of shelley he would miss
he believed in shelley's beauty and love.

3.

shelley's mother felt only failure and grief
she shared the despair of shelley's life
and how she felt as a mother
she had failed

she stood at the podium and wept for her failure.

4.

truth is found in both partner and mother
i do not know to which truth to attach myself
i think i grieve for them both and grieve for shelley
— if she had lived those in her world would be better off

she was once my sister's best friend
and i had seen both these sides of shelley
i smile and i feel sorrow
for shelley gave to others
without thought of her own grief.

5.

i am at a loss for another truth rises up in me
we cannot be where God is until we give up our lives here
and where we are God rarely comes to save the day
i do not know why this is but i am sure of it
based on the evidence i see

here at this funeral i feel that God is silent
and that it is we who must find the joy and beauty in life
without God's assurance

so i applaud shelley's partner
for bringing out the best in shelley for us to remember.

6.

goodbye shelley
as i listen to the two people who knew you best describe you
know that you have touched my life in a profound way
this day

i was in awe of the grief and the joy love can create in us
i believe all is well with you now
and it is we who must live with your passing.

To Chop Wood

should i chop wood today
or sit idle and dream of my soul
being set free from this kind of life?

if i chop wood i will be warm for the winter
if i dream of faraway places and contemplate the unknown
perhaps i will discover what ails my soul

do i choose a warm winter and risk unhappiness
or choose the search for my inner place of peace and the
cold?

> *of course i could contemplate and search for my inner self*
> *as i chop wood*
> *if it does not satisfy me then at least i tried*
> *and in this world of the vast unknown*
> *trial and error is the way*
> *as we are always at risk in searching for the right balance*
>
> *to think a simple chore like chopping wood*
> *has caused me to contemplate like this*
> *— though i would like to add more thoughts*
> *i am busy now chopping wood.*

The Snake Coiled

the snake coiled
i cowered

the birds screamed
the wind quieted

a cloud shadow moved over us
the rattler of the snake sang louder than the birds
then all was quiet

above me a hawk glided in the air
a predator looking for prey

as fate would have it the snake quickly disappeared
my nerves calmed i continued
to find the rest of the trail was safe

the hawk gradually became a dot on the horizon
the sun moved many shadow clouds through the sky

as i came to the trail's end i knew i would record this event
for one does not forget a coiled snake at one's feet so easily

> *my evident mortality on this trail does not assure me of*
> *God's presence*
> *though a hawk showed up in time to save the day*
> *and i am grateful*

> *but to whom am i grateful*
> *— the snake for disappearing*
> *the hawk for scaring the snake*
> *or perhaps to God for arranging it all?*

Terrorist in the Making

1.
wake me
before the
dawn

i have a
long journey
ahead

i am worn—
weary of
life

and i now must
fight my last
battle

i fear if i wake not
i might not wake
at all

wake me
before the
dawn

lest i fall
and miss my
destiny

my God
waits

2.
i have a
mission before
i rest

i must tell
the earth
what i have
been
through
before i
lay my
head one
more time
on my
pillow

i must take
other lives
with me
to this
next world
as a witness of our
struggle

i must leave
this world with a
victory

i cannot live
another
day
as

my God waits.

Longer Ways to Truth

1.

it is not time to be timid
the world goes on without us

it is a long way to truth
why not start our journey now?

it is only when we imagine a requirement by God
that we create a longer journey to God than is necessary

the journey will improve and be shorter
if we treat others as we want them to treat us

the journey will be longer and harder
if we build buildings where we must enter on our knees.

2.

religion is only a name
for a route to God that we have made
if this route turns out to be a longer way to God
perhaps more kindness and genuine mutual respect
will shorten it.

The Copper Trail

1.

i am hot and dusty
i am dry and cracked

i am sand and rock
i am root and clay

i am a vein of earth
i am called ore

i am called rich
i am called percent

i am hand dug
i am dynamited

i am underground
i am an open pit

i am mules and truck
i am bucketfuls

i am sifted
i am shafted

i am fired
i am molten

i am melted
i am poured

i am many generations
i am many families

i feed and give
i starve and take

i am towns
i am banks

i am bosses
i am unions

i am jewels
i am bracelets

i am crowns
i am ornaments

i am knives
i am spears

i am many arrowheads
i am many weapons

i am many languages
i am no language

i am no mind
i am mined

i am of no soul
i am owner of souls

i am of earth
i am of worth

where i lead
you follow.

2.

you may have what you find
i promise nothing more

welcome traveler
i am the copper trail

i was discovered before bibles
i was traded with gold and silver

i was guarded and hidden away
men died for me and kept me safe

if you follow after me
i am the copper trail

i do not talk so talk to yourself
i am not good company

i make companies
if you serve me well

keep your eye on the treasure
i am the copper trail

many cultures and nations and tribes
and governments have depended upon me

i am the desire for war
i make enemies out of friends and treaties with thieves

i have many stories to tell
i am the copper trail.

This Is for All the Fans

it started like any other day
— the sun rose
but before
the sun had set
every day
thereafter
would forever
be different
and it happened before
history could blink an eye

happy resurrection day

for all the fans of Jesus
aka the Son of God
i value any belief that can bring us
some peace on earth

happy resurrection day.

Tit for Tat

Late one night a man reached the corner where a rather voluptuous, not so young, woman stood.

The man was appalled. How was it that this woman would be standing at the corner at such a late hour?

The man felt compelled to impart this rude remark: "If you're selling, I am not buying."

The woman was horrified at such presumption. She looked at the man, then looked him up and down, then replied, "If you're buying, I am not selling."

To Linger On

1.
the sun is going down
and i have chores
to finish

but i linger to watch
the sun go behind
the hills

the colors in the sky
hold me in awe
as i stand

and stare for a moment
my thoughts straying
from the chores
of the day

if i never took the time to linger
i believe i would not be the
same person i am today.

2.
to linger and observe nature
or to entertain a thought
is the power of the linger
which can change us

i am a better person
because i have taken
time to linger at a scene
or in a thought

and if i had not lingered
i would not be here now
recording this part
of my life.

3.
perhaps it is the poet in me
that must pursue the linger
as if the choice is more of a
surrender than learning how

i will go now to finish my evening chores
and after that i will reflect more upon
this thought of lingering.

A Lesson Learned

the wind was picking up
a thunder cloud was forming
the beach sand whirled around us
as the sun set its light in all shades and colors

we picked up our picnic of sharp cheddar
smoked chub and bread and red wine
and hurried over the sand hill to the parking lot to the car

as we topped the hill i stopped to linger at the scene we
were leaving behind
i gave it a few more moments and that made a difference
in my memory of that day
—now a permanent snapshot in my mind.

There Is No Thought

there is no thought
i would withhold
or dream
i would not
tell

i would change any
thing that was
important
to you

the smile you give me
is worth all that
i can give.

What Is Your Opinion

the deception was the best i had ever seen
he loved her for sure but he also lusted

some say it was his dark side
that his behavior did not mean he did not truly love
only his wife.

others say he was a schemer and a liar
and that he used his wife and others to his advantage
to live as he wanted to live.

Part Two:
Another Lesson

A Day Hike

walking stick in hand
worn hiking boots fitted well to my feet
i start my hike

i have planned it for weeks
i have mapped it out
yet the first step i took landed me on the ground
having slipped on some loose gravel

— i had not planned that

though my pride was hurt i rose and dusted myself off
and then continued the hike

in fact there was very little on that hike that went
as planned

but despite all that i allowed myself to enjoy
the day anyway

heedless of mosquito bites and a sunburned head from
not positioning the headband over the top of my head
correctly and slipping on loose ground several times

how blind i am
how gracious my attitude
pretending to accept that my plans go wrong
i feel the fear rise in me
as i see this flaw in myself
and i wonder if i would be so gracious
when plans go wrong if they involved more serious issues

how easily we are fooled by our own strength
when we use lesser events
to judge ourselves on more serious ones.

Healing for Regret

1.
being grateful for what i have
is like a seed of humility that needs planting
a seed i hope can provide healing for my regrets.

2.
i have had many regrets
but as i learn the why and how of them
they begin to fade and i slowly begin to heal.

3.
humility has become my friend
and its discernment my guard

i change because i am willing to seek the friendship of
humility and all that comes with it.

4.
perfection is not the goal
rather —
humility as a guard
for my behavior
before i make
a move.

A Lesson in Learning

i looked into the eyes of a cow
and i saw its soul

i thought to myself
i can be friends with this cow

i wondered if the cow looked into my eyes and saw my soul
whether it would come to the same conclusion

somehow i do not think so
because i am the one ordering the steak.

Admit It

I read a beautifully written story about how a young couple survived a tornado.

They wrote how God heard their prayers that night and led them through the storm.

Then they each gave a history of their Christianity and how their parents were a vital part of their faith in Jesus and God.

They shared a long and articulate prayer of how God loves and cares for those who believe in Him and how He will answer their prayers.

this kind of belief in God is well and fine
but the millions of unanswered prayers
by the many people who have as much faith
— and perhaps more than this couple
— reveal otherwise

stories of "God's intervention" at best are random.

The Squirrel-in-the-apple-tree Theology

1.

the missing link
i think
is that Gods are Gods
animals are animals
and humans are humans

it seems animals fit the earth better than humans
Gods fit the spiritual better than humans
humans do not fit well in either realm
— groping for both worlds and disturbing them both

we possess what the animals and the Gods do not
an evil that wants what the animals and the Gods have
— without restraint

the conclusion is that our best hope for meaning
is wrapped up in the idea that we are known by the
animals and the Gods and ourselves through our deeds

and if we bare any good deeds at all it will be through
learning to treat all life as valuable

> *why are we burdened with learning*
> *what the animals and Gods do not need to learn?*

2.
i saw a squirrel in an apple tree
i thought the squirrel was looking at me
as if he wanted to tell me something
but i was too busy to notice
for i was looking up to the sky toward God

how irrelevant our theology is when we do not know how
to communicate with the animals or God

where are we from?
why are we stuck on answers that insist we are neither
from the animals or the Gods?

are either the animals or the Gods interested in us at all?

Blessed

Those who show mercy are blessed because they know how to show it and are an example for us all.

Those who are gentle in spirit are blessed because they draw us to them, causing us to want a gentle spirit of our own.

Those who seek righteousness are blessed because they have found the fortitude and courage to stand for truths that make a difference.

Those who are pure in spirit are blessed because they can see what is unseen and act as lights to help us all better see what is ahead.

anyone can learn mercy
become gentle in spirit
stand for righteousness
and see what is ahead.

Coexistence

I watched the squirrels and the quail quarrel for possession of the mesquite bush in my backyard.

Or I should say it looked like a quarrel to me, since I do not know their thoughts of the incident.

Despite their bickering back and forth, though, it does seem that they had a better sense of how to coexist than we.

Why is it that we feel superior to the squirrels and quail when it is we who are so needy . . . and it is they who can live through many winters without being much of a burden—in fact, without being any burden at all?

Side by side the squirrels and quail live through the seasons with no need for government or weapons for war, coexisting well enough for us to leave them alone.

If there is a lesson here it could be as simple as learning to coexist in order to decrease our need for so much government and so many wars.

Maybe tomorrow I will get up the nerve to ask the squirrels and quail for their take on the situation.

Copy That

1.

The auditorium was full, about five thousand people; the clapping and hand raising and hallelujah screams made the music barely audible.

Picking out the real content of the preacher's message you'd find only ten minutes' worth, but his oratory took two hours, one of which was spent on the sales pitch for our money.

2.

When someone asks for our money and demands our loyalty in the guise of God's message, I am disappointed, to say the least.

if i were rude i'd say the scene was nothing more
than nonsense

It is more profitable for my soul to seek to see us as equals than spend my time and money to support those who have very little to say and even less to offer in that way, and who only wants me for my money and allegiance to them.

i have to admit that kindness
truthfulness and mutual respect
are much better sermons
than the words of that preacher i heard that night

copy that?

Foundations for Friendships

we threw away years of good times
and memories over differences
in our beliefs in God

though we trusted each other
and never did one another harm

> *we threw our friendship away over whether or not Jesus is*
> *the Son of God*

what if we build our friendships on a different foundation
one that is not based on believing in God in the same way?

> *what if we agreed that to value each other*
> *as equal in the eyes of God*
> *and to treat each other's belief in God*
> *as equal in value to our own*
> *is the way to do no harm?*

is this not a better start for a friendship than having to
agree on Jesus?

God Is Much Better

If I were to believe in the basic theology of the Evangelical Christians I would see no real trust I could have in God.

I would not feel protected or loved, but betrayed — as the world suffers as prayers go unanswered.

I know this because I have been there, and because I know that the lack of evidence of a loving, caring God who is involved in our everyday lives is chilling.

I know this because the promise of the Evangelical Christian is that God intervenes for all who believe as they do, but I also know their proof of God is no more valid than any other.

Our failure to understand God does not disprove God, but only our understanding of Him.

The evidence shows that God does not intervene in the affairs of people in the way most Evangelical Christian doctrines describe.

take some time to pause and look at the reality of all the unanswered promises

then seek to know God on God's terms.

Look into the Eye of Your God

look into the eye of your image of God
and there you will see your own

look further in and you will see
how you want your salvation to be

though we are a creation of God
is it we who create an image of God for ourselves?

i have never heard reliable testimony
by those who claim they have gone to heaven and returned

i must make my own peace with God
and form an image of God i see best

i think God prefers it this way over
revealing Himself to us

> *with so many images and so few truths*
> *if God keeps His distance from us in this way*
> *then why would He give us the burden*
> *of demanding we find the one and only*
> *true image of Himself?*

Many Paths to One Truth

1.

my perspective is there are many paths to God
perhaps as many paths as there are people

in my view there is one truth upon which all paths rely
— to become a better human being

when i see that happening i believe it is evidence
we are getting closer to God

my path shows me that a single act of kindness
and concern for others is greater than
any loyalty to a religion

and it is the best foundation upon which to build
my beliefs.

2.

if i am tolerant and truly respectful of your spiritual beliefs
as being equal to my own
then i know i am getting closer to God

> *it is here i will light my evening fire*
> *it is here i will make my bed*
> *it is here i will find my shelter*

> *it is this path that will lead me home*
> *and it is the path that will make me a better human*

> *it is this path the leads me*
> *to peace in living and*
> *in dying.*

Bear Mountain Road, 1973

my muscles moved in harmony
as i enjoyed my afternoon run
i was in shape
i was 19

the sun was at 4:00 pm and the air still
the temperature about 75
the shadows of the trees could be seen

i knew this trail into the national forest well
it went for miles and miles and i jogged it often

one and one half miles in and one and one half miles out
that was my routine along with my roommate's
beagle — patches — who always came along

this one day the ravens circled above me
i offered up a few cawing sounds of my own
and then forgot all about them

it was as i was returning from my jog
and about 300 yards from the house
when a raven suddenly dived at me
and then two more joined the rush
and then several more

too surprised to wonder long at this event
my natural survival instinct kicked in
and backing myself up against a tree i picked up a branch
and began swinging

patches was between my legs wailing
i was screaming
and the ravens were cawing and swooping down on me

soon the birds began landing on the tree against which i
had backed
reaching for me with their beaks and claws

but suddenly there was silence all around me
the ravens had gone
leaving me stunned and afraid

there was no time to contemplate though
i had to move quickly
to run through the meadow
that last 300 yards to the house

i ran as hard as i could hoping the ravens would not return
but again they were swarming around me as i galloped
with patches between my legs howling all the way

my roommate was standing outside witnessing the event
i ran past him without a hello and did not stop running
until i was inside with the door firmly closed

my roommate followed — patches still at my heels
we watched the ravens land around the house to perch
until finally they gave up
and gradually dispersed

i don't caw at ravens anymore.

Story of a Conversation I Heard

An old man talking out loud to himself said, "I stayed in this village all my life up until now, and when I was young I turned down a good job in the city along with a chance of going to school. I do not know what I missed."

A young man who was listening to the old man replied, "I did leave the village to go to the city. I got a good job and an education, and now I have returned to the village, and I know what I have missed."

A waitress overhearing the conversation commented to the old man, "I do not think you missed anything. It has been here all along, and this young man is telling us that we are not missing a thing. I never left the village either."

The old man thought for a moment and then replied, "Maybe I haven't missed it, but perhaps it is that I could not see it. But I hope now I am able to hear what is being said because I do not want to miss the rest of this life that I cannot see."

The Human Design

1.

Though the human design is intricately assembled and awesome, it is also the worst designed creation ever.

The body, mind, and heart are so full of flaws that it is a wonder to even think we are made in the image of God.

2.

setting aside the idea of our destructive nature
— which in itself is a design flaw

we are in fact full of cancers and tumors and defects
and all kinds of mental and emotional illnesses
— it is obvious we are a design catastrophe.

3.

What does God have to say for Himself? My guess is not much, given his silence, a clear indication to me that He takes full responsibility and holds us not liable for our flaws.

Three Gods

1.
God is where many gods exist.

There is a god of the wind to cause a storm or a gentle breeze.

There is a god of the sky to cause seasons of abundance or droughts and tragedy.

There is a god of the earth to cause weeds and thorns or a variety of fruit and wheat.

There is a god of the humans, a god of the animals and a god of the heavens.

2.
Why is God where we imagine ourselves — at the center of God's universe?

Are we free to imagine God any way we please?

Or if we do not get it right are we to be punished by Him?

What is it in us that reasons that God is offended by us?

I do not think we can offend God, because God is God . . . and we are His creation.

I believe God is aware of all that that means.

3.
I came upon a wounded traveler and stopped to give him aid. Later I remembered the story of the good Samaritan and wondered at the wisdom of the truth of the feeling one experiences when helping another.

Is God where we see someone in need and we reach out to help?

I feel the act of helping another is possibly the closest to God we can get in the flesh, and it is possibly the most real form of worship — which cannot be replaced by any building, or ritual, or doctrine, or theology.

4.

Or . . . is "God" a word that explains the unexplainable and then *when we are able to explain it, it ceases to be God?*

Many Paths

I have met enough compassionate people in my life to know they did not all learn compassion the same way.

The testimonies of all these people from different cultures, religions, times, and circumstances bear witness to the fact that compassion can come through many paths.

How Long Does Beauty Last

Perhaps when two people are in love and age together, this is when beauty lasts.

Perhaps when beauty embraces love, and when time is added to the equation, this is when beauty becomes timeless.

I know couples like this and they are wonderful to watch.

Human Parts

— human will . . .
the part of us that can defy the odds of a most
probable failure

— human faith . . .
the part of us that reaches out and conceives the reality of
the unseen existence

— human spirit . . .
the part of us that was made to guide
our minds
hearts
and bodies.

When We Fall

1.

i believe

. . . that i saw the Son of God falling from his cross and God was there to catch him

. . . that like all humans who want to be Gods sooner or later we fall

. . . that Jesus fell because his name could not be God's and that God caught him and held him not guilty for claiming to be God

. . . that the good news is that God is here to catch us all and there is no crime we can commit on earth that will send us to a place called Hell

. . . that God has no anger toward His creations.

2.

i believe

. . . that more than likely Jesus did not claim of himself what we claim of him

. . . that Jesus brought us great and profound reflections concerning a way for us to coexist . . . and that in those words Jesus brought us good news that places no man higher than another

. . . that Jesus' good news was in his teachings.

3.

i believe

. . . that all writings of a heaven and a hell and of a man
who is a God who has to die for our crimes only cause us
to become prejudiced toward any who believe differently
i also believe this is not good news to bring to the world
that kind of God

. . . that there is no act for which God would require any of
us to be punished eternally or require blood of Himself or
others to be spilled in order to make us clean enough for
heaven

. . . that God has not given us such a burden nor does He
have the need to burden His creation with the fear of a hell
after death

. . . that God approves of us the way we are.

4.

i believe

. . . that the more human Jesus is the better understood his
words are

. . . that the mercy of God treats all humans the same
when it comes to our entrance into the next life

. . . that if God sees us as equals as we enter into the next
life we should value each other as equals in this one

. . . that although i cannot prove this view of equality is
true it is a better way for us to live on this earth

. . . that if faith has no need of proof other than itself
then beliefs and faith must be seen for what they are

. . . that if we all go to heaven and God is pleased to grant
that to us then our flaws are God's responsibility and not
ours

. . . that we could be more at peace with where we go after
we die and more conscious of the good and the harm of
our behavior if we believe God approves of us all.

5.
i believe

. . . that God will catch us all for His mercy is
unconditional for us all

. . . that there is no theology or doctrine or creed or church
or sanctuary or temple needed
if you want one then make one but God's mercy is
sufficient with or without them.

6.
i am grateful to have the image of Jesus falling from the
cross so i can see his teachings better and i can appreciate
him more as a human

> *jesus if i have offended you by lifting you higher*
> *than you are*
> > *forgive me*
> *and if you have lifted yourself up higher*
> *than you are*
> > *i forgive you*
> *you are much better as a human from birth till death*
> > *and beyond*

you are as we are and you showed us a better way
to coexist
        i am forever grateful to you
and the same God who caught you as you fell is there
to catch me as well.

Who Would Believe?

"murderer!" the people yelled, "murderer!"

months later he was convicted of murder and received the
death penalty

a prison minister came to this man and explained Christ to
him and "heaven" and "hell"

the man prayed for God to forgive him so he would not be
punished eternally for the murder he committed

the man went to the electric chair a few years after
receiving Christ in his heart
— he was at peace

I believe this man went to heaven. I believe that
once there he saw many people and heard so many
different beliefs that he was stunned to think that God
was so merciful as to accept all these beliefs as worthy of
heaven. . . . Stunned to think that though these people did
not believe as the prison minister believed, they had all
gone to heaven. But it mattered little to the man now that
the prison minister had been wrong, for to know of the
great mercy of God now was the most wonderful news
of all. And though he did not know of it until he got to
heaven, right and wrong in this way was no longer of any
consequence.

Just knowing that everyone he knew would also be
in heaven was wonderful news as well, for anyone who
knew of this heaven and God's mercy would know that
there was no hell and no possibility that anyone would be
turned away from heaven.

Cannot we conceive of a God this merciful . . . or is believing in a God like this asking too much of faith?

It's Personal

cannot we believe
spiritual beliefs
are better served
if we keep
them personal?

cannot we respect
another's right
to that?

cannot we view
our behavior as proof
of our spiritual beliefs?

> *or is this asking*
> *too much?*

Lesson on Beliefs

a belief is only a belief
it has no regard for how insistent we are
that it is the truth

the truth about a belief is
that it is a belief.

Lesson on the Use of the Word Choice

If we believe that it is up to us to believe in God in the way we choose, then the idea of a Hell that waits for those who choose wrong is not a choice, but in fact an ultimatum forced on our free will.

So, the idea that we have a choice is suddenly overtaken by the idea that we are punished for the wrong choice.

Therefore, when we use the word "choice" in conjunction with the theology of Heaven and Hell it becomes like a hammer to our heads.

In my way of thinking, if such an important place as Hell exists, God would have made it much more clear and not left it up to a matter of choice. I would therefore have to say that "choice" is a poor choice of words.

Furthermore, why our fixation with Heaven and Hell, with the idea that mercy is only granted to those who make the right choice of how to believe in God, and the idea that all the rest of us go to Hell or somewhere less than those who chose "correctly"?

Pay Attention

when questions arise it's time to pay attention

why is it difficult for us
to show mutual respect and tolerance
for any belief that harms not others?

is it not possible that all approaches to God
are equal and that all have their successes
and failures?

could it not be that our beliefs are our own
and therefore full of failures?
after all
we are speaking about us — humans

why could it not be
that God works with all beliefs
and all failures —
after all
we are speaking about God.

The Way of Oral Historic Scriptures

I do not think the writers really knew what the ancient prophets, leaders, and spiritual masters actually said as they began to record these oral traditions, beliefs, histories, and revelations, but I do believe that by the time the writing was finished those scribes believed they knew without a doubt what the ancient figures believed and meant by their words.

why is it that when we write down our histories and beliefs we believe it is supposed to keep everyone else from having the freedom to present a different view of those events and beliefs?

Friendship Lost

i realized —
the friendship was lost
i was a passenger on his raft and he was the captain

so one day i disembarked at the dock
for i could not be friends in this way longer

i pushed —
his raft away from the dock
and watched as my friend drifted down the river

i saw —
that we had been friends as he'd seen fit for many years
and that it was time for me to get off

time has passed —
where i am more content not having a friendship
that is only possible if it means riding on another's raft

i miss the friendship —
i do not miss his raft.

Part Three:
Dream Quiz

Forest Called Truth

I dreamed there was a forest called truth, and that there were many who ventured there.

Upon my entrance into this forest I saw wondrous trees and plants and animals and flowers of all kinds.

I thought about all the beauty that truth holds for us to discover, and was grateful for this forest.

As I ventured farther I stumbled on a castle made from the trees of the woods; as magnificent as the castle was, however, it sent a chill through me.

How long can a forest survive when people take truth and do with it as they please without considering the consequences they have caused?

How does a forest allow us to partake of its treasure but does not stop the thief, as if to say "Any who find truth may do with me as they wish?"

— but is it only the wise who see Me as the essence of life?

The Poet's Dreams

to see what is not seen
and to dream what others cannot

to accept what is unacceptable
and to not accept what is acceptable

to dream of distant lands that exist not
and to question paradises that do

> *poets are the sanity of the paradox*
> *and the insanity of the norm*

days and nights are different for poets
the need to express on paper inexplicable

but to readers theirs is a much needed voice
and civilization would be less without them

so i celebrate the poet's dreams
and all that poets savor from their dreams

like letters from a place we can only imagine
through the poet's eyes.

We Delight in the Name of the Lord (a dream)

we meet in the air
for battle
my spiritual warriors
and i
for there is a war in
the heavens
where an enemy lives
and breathes

i have been invited
by the angels
to fight alongside
them and with
God

after the battle is won
we gather
on the earth
around a great fire

we circle the fire
and sing
the victory song
we sing
these words over
and over
till the arrival
of dawn

> *we delight in the name of the Lord*
> *we delight in the name of the Lord*
> *we delight in the name of the Lord*

we circle with our backs
to the fire
unable to look upon each
other's wounds

as we sing
our wounds begin to heal
and our hope for a better
life is restored

> *an enemy defeated*
> > *brings out the joy in us all*
> *and to have the heavens*
> > *at our side*
> *is a joy unspeakable*
> > *and a rest only dreamed of*

i awaken from this dream
rested and yet tired
as if i have been there and
experienced it all
—the song on my lips
as i open my eyes

> *we delight in the name of the Lord*
> *we delight in the name of the Lord*
> *we delight in the name of the Lord.*

Trails (1)

1.

i see trails everywhere
many of which i would not follow

wherever we go we leave a trail
and at times i would not follow my own

these trails are the prints our behavior leaves
on other humans and every other living thing

> *joy sadness peace anger*
> *truthfulness deceit kindness*
> *bitterness compassion*
> *aloofness generosity*
> *greed selflessness*
> *respect*
> *— we leave all kinds of trails.*

2.

I watch an elderly man walk by me one afternoon, his
bearing wise and gentle and kind.

I watch him step to the side as two boys run briskly
across his path.

I see him pick up an item left by a family on a car as
they walk away, and then catch up with the family and
hand them the item.

I see his trail as he disappears around a corner and am
encouraged by what I see. I want the same bearing he has
for myself.

I think his trail is of the spirit; other trails I see are of
the flesh.

my spirit unblemished
my counselor from God
my flesh burdened in mind
heart and body seeks
for a God it can trust —
i am here.

3.
i make a trail now to my spirit
where no confession or
loyalty to a church or synagogue
or mosque can be —

we are on our own
when it comes to
making
trails.

Trails (2)

1.

what is this trail behind me?

> *my words and my deeds*
> *leave evidence of my journey*
> *i make friends and i make enemies*
> *by the kind of trails i make.*

2.

my flesh wants to know

> *do i leave greed and deceit*
> *and harm wherever i go*
> *or do i leave compassion*
> *respect and truthfulness?*

3.

what kind of trail do i leave?

> *the spirit judges correctly*
> *for it offers only nonjudgmental paths*
> *and the flesh judges selfishly*
> *for it considers anyone a possible adversary.*

Falling

i dreamed i was falling through the air — no sky — just air
and thought to myself if i do not wake myself i will keep falling

i awakened and remembered that as i was falling
i was debating with myself about how faith was meant to be used
and i saw i was falling because my faith was creating
a false reality

i was without a way in to finding faith
and i was without a way out of this dream.

A Way In

is faith our attempt to move God
and is reality what happens?

is reality more close to God than faith?

is reality only undisputed evidence
and faith the denial of reality?

is reality the *way in* to the real
search for God?

A Way Out

is faith for the passage from this life to the next?
is reality the truth about what God does and does not?
does peace mean coming to terms with reality and faith?

i dream of the day we have these answers
but i do not want to dream for it too much
for i may find myself falling out of my dream
with no way back in.

Notes on the Mind's Eye

1.

though i visit the place of my mind's eye often
i am a stranger there

do i go to my mind's eye or does it come to me?
is it waiting to be aroused or does it arouse?

the way i see it —
my mind's eye sees me and i see it
and any wisdom arrived therein
is my own contemplation
which would not be
without having made contact.

2.

dark is darker there
if i perceive the darkness
then i see the light

the unknown is all around me there
if i surrender to the unknown
then it is willing to open to me

paths are revealed there
i know i must choose one
for my mind's eye does not choose for me.

3.

i look into the eye of my God
where i see my own image

i look further into the eye of my God
and there i see my own salvation
i look further still to see if i can see
my own death and afterlife

i learn that the eye of God
reveals everything to us in its due time

and it is we who imagine we see it
before its time.

Meadow Creek and You

i am three miles down meadow creek
just past the falls
the shadow of the canyon walls
cools the heat off my neck

my mind is full of the past week
but it slowly empties
to where the only memory that lingers
is that of you

> my return from meadow creek
> is much quicker
> the sun casts shadows
> and the colors melt into one another

> in rhythm with all the sounds
> of the forest and creek
> i make my way along the canyon
> seeing you in my mind's eye

> i smile because in a few hours
> i will be home again

> *as i lie in bed and think of the afternoon hike*
> *i am also thinking of you with me*
> *walking meadow creek trail*
> *and gradually fade off into sleep.*

My Eyes Search for You

        1.
my eyes search for yours
and a glimpse
is all it takes

with the right look
we give each other our loyalty
and our love

then my imagination takes over
and i create an image of you
beautiful inside and out.

        2.
i dreamed of you last night
and i watched you by firelight
you cast a shadow
in the movements of the flame

i watched you undress
your silhouette showed your beauty
you were quiet and contemplative
and at ease with yourself

you were taut
well defined
confident
at peace
and well cared for

i watched you till the light of the fire dimmed
i desired you as i always have
and before i woke i saw you
see me watching you
then our eyes met and you smiled.

3.

as the dream fades i reach over
to touch you my wife
and the memory of you this night
gives me peace

i slip back into sleep.

Part Four:
Of Teachings (1)

Author's Note: I have read that the symbol "Z" (or the zigzag) is a common Native American symbol and motif (as recognized by the Native Plains peoples of North America). As I remember it, if the center line of the Z slants left, it indicates the path of the soul — the journey the spirit takes and the walk one makes within the spirit. If the center line of the Z slants to the right, it indicates the forces that call loudly to a person's soul — passions or issues that compel a person to choose a certain path in life.

The two horizontal lines (top and bottom, connected by the middle slant line) indicate our life's journey, the understanding we obtain while on the earth, and the realization of the "life of sky" (available at whats-your-sign.com). My interpretation of the sky and earth is that they represent the spirit and the flesh.

God Is Pleased

1.
the usual way . . .
i come to God
in need
for it is food
shelter and safety
i seek

i bow and bring
offerings and
prayers and
tithes

what i cannot do
for myself
i ask
You to do
on my behalf

i believe if my
offerings and
prayers please
You then
You will fill my needs.

2.
another way . . .
You have formed me
placed in me a spirit
without flaw

though my body
heart
and mind
are burdened

You have ordained
my spirit to be
as counselor
if i find my spirit
i find You

You are
always there
all the day and
all the night.

    3.
God's way . . .

God welcomes us all
none is turned away
come as you are

God is God
and cannot be offended
no need does God have
of hell

all spirits return
to God
while our
bodies
minds
and hearts
remain forever on earth.

4.
the path way . . .

God is pleased with us
for God has made us

God sides with no one
against another

our quarrels are our own

God offers us counsel
by way of our spirits

and we must fight our
own fights

God is not partial.

5.
the free way . . .

no offerings does God need
no prayers does God need
no tithes does God need

God is here

God is pleased
with what He
has made.

Chose the Path

1.

i chose my path and its worth is determined
by my actions and my deeds

if i walk the hills in the mornings and evenings
and worship God there
if i go to the scriptures that speak to me
and worship God there
if i go to the sanctuaries built by us
and worship God there
if i burn incense and wear robes
and worship God as I do
if i sing loudly and clap to God —

> *what reward have i if my worship leads me not*
> *to value all humans as equal to myself?*

2.

if there are many paths to God
then God is great enough to guide anyone who
seeks Him —

> *the paths we choose determine how we relate to each other*
> *and how we believe God relates to us.*

If We Knew

if we knew what our souls sought from God
then we would seek our spirits
for God is there

and that is where our souls find rest
and their burden is lightened.

How Do We Know

How do we know when to make war and when to seek peace?

Do we knock first on our enemy's door with peace offerings, or do we wait till our enemy knocks on our door with war offerings?

Before we respond, consider that . . .

War fought in self-defense seeks peace and resolution, whereas preemptive war makes an enemy for life, and war fought in self-defense seeks to preserve what is ours, whereas those who seek to conquer have no regard for the life of their prey.

So beware of the arrogance of victories . . .

Because though our lives are better because of a victory in war, what we do not have is the knowledge of a victory without war . . . and that is the failure of all victories.

My Confession

my life is my worship
and my worship is my life

i know God by how i live
i know God by how i rest.

Choose One

Before my birth there were two entities knocking on the door of my soul. I inquired of them to tell me who they were.

One said, "I am known as the killer of my enemies."

The other said, "I am known as the harmony with all that lives."

And then a third voice said, "Choose one."

i believe we are known by God and others
by how we choose to confront an enemy.

Live Forever

use the land
care for the land
and leave the land
as you found it
or better than you found it

take what you need
leave what you do not need

the bear and elk and wolf and birds
have need of the land as well

do this and you and the animals
will live forever
and generations after you will have plenty.

The Spirit Guides

1.

body—search my depths
heart—search my depths
mind—search my depths
till you find my spirit.

2.

spirit—counsel my body
and mind and heart
breathe life into them
so they will know
where to find
compassion
conscience
wisdom
courage
and strength.

Harmonies

1.

If I seek harmony with my neighbors and enemies it does not necessarily mean we will be friends, but rather that I will respect our differences and expect that we can live according to our beliefs without interference from the other.

Maybe this is the way mutual trust is formed, whereby we honor another's way. However, the problem is that my neighbors and enemies may see my presence as a threat.

History shows us that we are all guilty of accusing others of what we ourselves have done and not done as well.

This is the most difficult of harmonies: to judge another without any effort toward coexistence.

2.

In a small community where harmony exists based on similar beliefs, it is easy to think we have answers for all the world. But the more people who are involved, the more difficult it is to maintain the harmony.

3.

One person's view of harmony may not be another's, so how can we find a way to coexist? How can we agree on the element of basic human rights?

No matter how wise we are for ourselves and no matter how able we are to live in harmony, we may not be wise enough to guide a people and culture we do not know.

4.

We have not ever arrived at real community harmony, for the ones in power are not interested and humans are not naturally prone to be selfless.

Sides and Wars

1.

If God does not involve Himself in our quarrels, then why would God lead us into victory? If there must be war, pray for guidance, wisdom, courage, and strength.

> *why do we believe God takes sides —*
> *as if to say that God creates us*
> *then becomes an enemy*
> *to His own creation.*

2.

If God does not involve Himself in our quarrels, then our wars defeat our created purpose, for I believe we desire life without wars.

Why are we so naive to believe our side is God's side?

Why are we so naive to believe there is a kind of war where we defend God's plan for us on earth?

> *for as much as God does not take sides in our wars*
> *God also allows us to destroy each other.*

3.

Is there a way to have peace without war?

Is the question worth seeking, though an answer has yet to be found?

In My Soul

1.

i believe . . .
that beyond the boundaries of belief
lies the truth of our beings

boundaries that want no more truth than their own
are the makers of all wars and all justification.

2.

i believe . . .
that if we do not want to be lied to
cheated or oppressed
enslaved or harmed unjustly

then we should be unwilling
to lie or cheat
oppress or enslave
and harm unjustly

and that valuing others as equal
to ourselves is often espoused
but rarely applied.

3.

i believe . . .
that to learn to coexist on the earth before we leave it
would offer us one of the greatest truths.

Part Five:
Ty Teachings (2)

Perspective

I see it differently from you; is that wrong?

Tolerance

worship how you choose
all that I ask is that you do not intrude
upon my worship.

Intolerance

i am intolerant of behavior that oppresses
steals
lies
manipulates
harms
enslaves.

Connection

connection to God is impossible to explain
it is best to experience it rather than explain it

connection to God is impossible to teach
it is best to experience it rather than teach it

connection to God is to experience God
where no explanation or teaching can go.

Belief

The reality of belief is knowing it seeks to convince us of a truth, but without being tested it means nothing.

Compassion

Compassion is my compass to God.

Patience

Patience is one of the most sought after arts of life, but the least practiced.

The proof of patience is not the waiting; rather, it is the fruit that the waiting produces.

Though patience may not always give us what we have waited for, it can give us a strength that can heal us from defeats and keep our victories in their rightful place.

The first sign of patience is listening.

Not knowing how to listen is the first clue to the absence of patience.

Patience may not necessarily guarantee moral character; it is up to us to add this to patience.

Doubt

Doubt is a reasonable view of truth. Without doubt
I would not know how to question and wrestle with truth.

Fear not any questions or doubt; rather let them come,
for questions and doubt can lead us to better truths.

Fear not doubt, but fear those who would condemn doubt
and those who fear it.

Humility

Humility is the confidence not to treat others unfairly;
humility sees everyone as equal and valuable to God.

Conscience

Conscience is one of the voices of the spirit. It does not force itself upon us; rather, it is we who must choose conscience.

Conscience brings to surface the evil and good within us and is servant to our free will.

New

Discovery and invention are not always for the better; discernment is required.

Knowledge is not always safe; it is up to us to make it so.

Defense

The right to self-defense is not taught; it comes from within. Therefore, God has placed it in us.

Duality of Good and Evil

The duality of good and evil is born in us and it will die
with us; therefore, it is a burden, and it is also our way
to mercy.

God accepts the blame for the good and evil in us, and
mercy is God's way to amend the harm that good and evil
have done to us.

Servanthood

Servanthood is an attitude whereby we value all life with the view that God created life.

God Is Able

come as you are
God approves

no approach to God is better than any other
the idea is to approach

God is bigger than any belief we could have about Him
we cannot offend God
only ourselves.

Religion vs. Spirituality

Though we may find spirituality in religion and religion in spirituality, neither needs the other to exist.

If religion seeks to connect with God, then we should hope God is willing to connect to our religion.

Spirituality and religion can be as different as light and dark; light can shine on darkness, and darkness can hide light.

If I seek God through religion, I hope I will always remember that religion is the vehicle and God the destination.

Part Six:
7 Teachings (3)

Historical Reflections of Southwest New Mexico

The Victorio Perspective

1.
the land and the sky
the animals that walk on earth
the birds that fly
are one . . .
and the chihenne apache are one

Ussen has made all and made all one

we are the people of harmony
our pursuit is harmony
with all that lives
on earth

the balance of all is in Ussen's hand

white painted woman gave
birth to child of the water
and *Ussen* made us to follow
child of the water forever

only Ussen sees the wisdom of creation

our ways are in the way *Ussen*
has made us

may *Ussen* grant us wisdom
courage and strength and compassion

may Ussen show us how to live in harmony with our enemies

we will sing by the warm springs
where life calls us to be

we were made to be warm springs apache
chihenne apache

> *Ussen made our spirits to sing to Ussen*
> *and to sing to our hearts and minds.*

2.
our mark is upon our land
wherever we sleep
wherever we drink
wherever we eat
the land is ours to use

> *we take what we need*

wherever we hunt
wherever we grow
wherever we marry
wherever we die

> *we take what we need*

we leave plenty
for all other living
creatures of earth

our mark is sacred
what we take is sacred
all that is created is sacred
the land of the warm springs apache is sacred

may my children and their children
as with my father and his father
know of Ussen and who Ussen is.

3. "Bi-duye" (Victorio)

Bi-duye
go to the mountain
and walk the ridge
and look in every direction
for your enemy comes and he is
the killer of enemies

Bi-duye
your days will not be like your fathers'
for their enemies were known
but yours is a new breed
and he wants what is yours

Bi-duye
i give into your hands
all weapons to defend
what is yours

i will never be far from reach
but i do not involve myself
in the quarrels of my creation

so pray that you can
see how to live with
the killer of enemies

Bi-duye:
go to the mountain
keep watch and pray
while white painted woman
and child of the water wait
for Ussen to answer

the days of
warm springs apache
are changing
and they will never be
as they were before.

4.
treaties made by people who have no respect for the land
are worthless
—like spoiled waters

the trash you see and the dead carcasses
that lie all around were not left by you
but by a people who wish to make treaties with you

they bring with them items to trade
that are meant to lure you away from the land
and make you lazy and dependent upon them
for your life

stay away from their trades
steer away from their camp
and live as you have for thousands of years
no good will come from these treaties

those who come with treaties and take without asking
and destroy without regard
come only with the intent of taking what is yours

beware of treaties made with a people
who live not as you do and who want you
not to live as you do.

    5. Ussen
Ussen:
i must travel this path
that my fathers have never traveled
and i must make treaties with people
who know us not and want not to know us

i fear the worst for we are so outnumbered
and now facing starvation
i have no hope but to trust those
who cannot be trusted

do i lead us into the sacred hills and die free
and leave no hope for my children
or do i lead us into slavery and die humiliated
but also go with hope for my children
to live for tomorrow?

Chiricahua Apache Woman

1.
her eyes were still
and steady and she stared
into mine . . .

or was she looking at me at all
i could not be sure
but why would she be staring at me?

chiricahua apache woman
what do you see?

did you see into my soul
or were you looking
past me?

my eyes were fixed upon her eyes
she smiled and then looked to the floor . . .

chiricahua apache woman
what do you see?

the clerk at the counter was patient
and waited for the woman to reach for the chocolate kisses
and hand him a five-dollar bill

as the woman took her change she looked at me
and then turned to the clerk
then looked again
this time at the floor

chiricahua apache woman
what do you see?

2.

later an elderly man told us about her
that she was known as a medicine woman
and kin to Cochise

he said she had a reputation
for seeing into the future and settling disputes

> *chiricahua apache woman*
> *what do you see?*

i wondered the rest of the day
if indeed she'd seen into me and into my future

she'd looked down after looking at me
as if to say *do not be alarmed — i was alerted*
but you will be ok

> *chiricahua apache woman*
> *what do you see?*

had this chiricahua apache woman focused on me
or had she merely looked in my direction
and not seen me at all?

does she really see into the soul
or does she only imagine she does —
we may never know

> *chiricahua apache woman*
> *what do you see?*

3.

in the land of the chiricahua
once roamed the apaches — free

we spent our weekend there
among the beautiful cottonwoods
that lined the river's edge

at times i believed i could spot a shadow
or a movement through those trees
as if the memory of the spirits of the chiricahua apaches
still breathed

and upon those hills i imagined
i heard their voices in the breeze
voices that would not leave

and because of this sense that pushed into my spirit
i have come to believe in the chiricahua apache
medicine woman i saw that day

> *did she know i would sense those spirits*
> *or did she send them my way?*

as the sun set over the hills
we made our way back east to silver city new mexico

the chiricahua apache woman
was fading in my mind
but i knew there was something about her
that would live with me forever.

> *chiricahua apache woman*
> *what did you see?*

Introduction to La Capilla

There was once a small chapel that sat upon the top of Chihuahua Hill in Silver City, New Mexico. The chapel was called La Capilla, Spanish for "The Chapel." As I remember the story, in 1887 residents of Silver City could look to the south of downtown and see the chapel, made of adobe bricks and timbers from nearby trees, at the top of the hill.

For several decades, La Capilla served as part of the community's religious activities, which included pilgrimages and festivals celebrating the Feast of Our Lady of Guadalupe. La Capilla contained a statue of the Virgin of Guadalupe, which came from Mexico. But, after some time had passed, the statue was returned to Mexico from where it came. Thus, the chapel was not used anymore for its primary purpose, and slowly the structure decayed.

Now, 110 years later, the residents of Silver City have supported the rebuilding of the chapel on the top of Chihuahua Hill, where it had originally stood and now stands as a beautiful reminder of our past.

Two sisters living in Silver City in the late 1880s funded the construction of La Capilla to house the statue of the Virgin of Guadalupe. It was the local Hispanic residents who built the chapel from adobe and wood. The story as to why the sisters wanted this structure built is still debated. Some say the structure was for penance, for the sisters may have been involved in prostitution. Historically, many cities like Silver City had their share of prostitutes, and the stories are very diverse as to why and how women entered that profession.

Whatever the original motivation for the building of La Capilla, it remained as a focal point of worship and solitude for the residents of the Chihuahua Hill area after it was no longer used by the Catholic Church.

Some say the chapel slowly deteriorated and the timbers were salvaged for other uses. La Capilla remained standing until a violent windstorm brought it down around the year 1918. By the early 1920s, the chapel was no longer standing; only the foundation remained as evidence of a structure ever being there at all. Many stories abound about La Capilla, one of which I will share here.

(ref: silvercity.org/still the old west/la capilla heritage park.php, La Capilla Heritage Park, Silver City New Mexico)

La Capilla

1.

A historical, small, one-room catholic church known as La Capilla sits at the top of a hill known as Chihuahua Hill in Silver City, New Mexico.

Originally, La Capilla was an adobe structure, its roof tin and tile wood beams held it all together, but why it was built is still debated.

Though it was abandoned for its original purpose, it was still used by the people of Chihuahua Hill who visited La Capilla regularly.

There is a story told of an old man who went to the chapel every Friday evening and sat outside. This man never went inside, for he had made a vow to God that he would wait for the murderer and rapist of his wife to return to the scene of the crime — the church.

One night, many years before when he was a young man and newly married, the man told his wife he was too tired to go to the chapel with her. He did this although a few years earlier he had promised he would go with his wife to the chapel every Friday night if she would marry him. Agreeing to his terms, the two were married.

Though it was Friday night now, and the couple's usual prayer time, the man's wife agreed to allow him to stay home this one night and went to the chapel alone to pray.

She never returned.

The young man became enraged at his wife's disappearance, blaming himself because he had broken his vow.

The story says that the man's wife was seen with several men that night and that her body was never found.

From that time on, the young man sat outside the chapel every night hoping his wife would return and that they would enter the chapel together—or that the men who had killed her would return and the grieving husband would be able to avenge his wife's death.

The man had vowed not to enter the chapel until he avenged his wife's death or she returned, for he felt God was punishing him for breaking his original vow.

As the years continued to pass, La Capilla slowly deteriorated, but the people who lived nearby still went there to pray.

And the man sat on the steps . . . waiting.

2.

After twenty years passed the young man had aged; now fifty he was an old man. But still he went to the chapel every Friday night and waited outside, keeping his vow.

One evening a young girl, barely thirteen, stopped by the chapel and asked him, the old man, to watch her goat as she went in to pray. When she entered the chapel he heard an unusual noise that sounded like a kick . . . and then all was quiet.

About ten minutes later two men briskly walked out of the church.

The old man knew something wrong had happened inside La Capilla, and so was faced with a dilemma. Did he dare go in to see what had happened—knowing if he went into the chapel it would mean breaking his vow before God?

The old man paced back and forth in front of the chapel, not knowing what to do, for it had been twenty years since his wife's disappearance.

But suddenly the man realized that if he let this young girl be harmed as he had his wife it would be worse than breaking a vow.

So the old man quickly entered the chapel where he found the young girl whom the men had attempted to rape. He saw that the girl had fought them. Although she had been badly beaten and was terribly bruised, she was alive.

The man helped the girl out of the chapel and walked her home, where he told her mother what had happened.

The mother informed the police and the girl was given medical attention.

The old man noted the ten children in the girl's home and the lack of a father, so before he left he chopped some wood for the family.

The next day there was a plate of fresh tortillas at the door of his tent with a note attached. It was from the mother of the girl he had helped, and said, "You have no home, no children and no wife of your own.

"I have no husband of my own. Perhaps if we give each other what the other one does not have, then God will bless us both and forgive us both for any crimes we might have done."

3.

Years later the grandchildren of this woman wrote letters to the city requesting La Capilla be restored.

Over the years many other letters besides theirs had been sent to the city requesting the same thing.

It took many years for this request to be honored, and many of the people who sent letters had stories about how La Capilla had played a part in their family history.

La Capilla was completely destroyed a few years after the attack of this thirteen-year-old girl.

Some say it was the wind that tore it down and some say it was God who destroyed the chapel because the penance of the two sisters was complete. Others say it was time and decay that caused the chapel to fall.

Whatever the reason, the chapel fell, until years later the city finally restored it again.

Stories like these are passed down; most are never written. This particular story reminds us to put pen to paper so we pass them on to the next generation, for it might have need of them.

4.

In the end, the old man accepted the woman's offer and he lived with her and her children in her house, doing the chores and helping with the needs of the neighbors until they both passed away.

The old man left a note at his death asking the priest to read it at his funeral. The note said,

> *"be careful what you vow to God*
> *for it can shape your life forever*
> *i think God does not hold us to vows*
> *that seek revenge or cause any of us harm*
> *i think a vow is only honored by God*
> *when it strengthens us to do good*
>
> *my vow of revenge nearly killed me and a young girl*
> *because i broke that vow i was able to save*
> *the girl and lift a weight off my own shoulders."*

Where Is the Wisdom

1.
where is the wisdom
and guidance that
God offers
when—

an adversary is determined
to destroy us no matter
how hard we try to
make peace?

do we become subservient
to this adversary and
hope that in time
they will change

or do we stand our ground
knowing that if we do not
then the adversary will
make short our time
on earth
or enslave us?

2.
do we live a slave or die free
—which is correct?

i hear the answer
and it is in the heart of each of us

i think indecision is the worst place
in this scenario

whichever we choose
we should search God for peace
without regret.

3.
so is it that God allows all people
to work out their own salvation to their own satisfaction
and approves?

is wisdom found within our own reasoning
as to whether or not any of us will fight or seek peace?
does God want us to search our own spirits
for the answer that is right for us?

— the wisdom we are permitted here by God
is a wisdom where we are required
to trust our spiritual beliefs
without any real definite answers from God.

Train without a Conductor

we are like passengers on a train without a conductor
though there is a track that keeps us on track
we never really see the conductor
so as passengers finding a sense of safety on the train can
be daunting

staying on the train and trusting the tracks can feel like
having no real control
as to our final destination

we must therefore make our way the best we can
within the confines of the train and track

> *eventually we all arrive at our destination*
> *believing we will see the conductor*
> *as we exit the train.*

Journeys End

all journeys end
it is how they end that takes my soul down this road

    my back is against the canyon wall
    my enemies do not want peace
    they want the soul of my people
    to end and never return

    i now wait for the dawn
    seeking *Ussen* to waken us
    so that we can find our own peace this day
    for when our arrows fail
    we must fall with honor
    at the feet of *Ussen*

    i will leave the earth with the hope
    that my children see a better day
    i fear not death or life
    only not making my peace with all
    that lives on the earth

    today i will join my fathers by the fire
    and wait with them for my children

    all journeys must end
    and it is how they end
    that takes my soul down this road
    and leads me to the final dawn
    that my eyes will see

one day we will all be together
where neither dawn nor dusk lead us
— only Ussen.

About the Author

Tony Prewit was born in Stamford, Texas in 1954 and then moved with his family at the age of eight to Silver City, New Mexico. He has earned both bachelor's and master's of arts degrees and has traveled extensively throughout the United States as a musician. Besides his interest in poetry, the author has written, directed, and performed in several plays and as a mime actor. In addition, he is an artist who delves in photography, charcoals, pastels, and watercolors. Art is his private therapy.

For over thirty-five years the author kept a journal of poetry that chronicled his most secret, inner struggles with his belief in God. During that time he lived what seemed to be a fairly normal life—traveling, going to school, marrying, and owning a retail furniture company. This journal, however, does not chronicle his "normal" life, but his struggles with belief. He believes many people have these same kinds of inner challenges with life, and this journal brings to the forefront the reality of these challenges.

Since 1978 he has lived with his wife Pat, a classical pianist, in Silver City, New Mexico, the place he considers home for its culture, land, seasons, and people.